NURSERY RHYMES

Illustrated by David Crossley

Brown Watson

ENGLAND

SING A SONG OF SIXPENCE

Sing a song of sixpence,
A pocket full of rye;
Four and twenty blackbirds
Baked in a pie.

When the pie was opened,
The birds began to sing;
Wasn't that a dainty dish
To set before the King.

The King was in his counting house
Counting out his money;
The Queen was in the parlour
Eating bread and honey.

The maid was in the garden
Hanging out the clothes;
When down came a blackbird
And pecked off her nose.

ROCK-A-BYE BABY

Rock-a-bye baby,
On the tree top,
When the wind blows
The cradle will rock.

When the bough breaks,
The cradle will fall -
Down will come baby,
Cradle and all!

MARY, MARY

Mary, Mary, quite contrary,
How does your garden grow?
With silver bells and cockle shells
And pretty maids all in a row.

RIDE A COCK-HORSE

Ride a cock-horse to Banbury Cross,
To see a fine lady upon a white horse;
Rings on her fingers and bells on her toes,
She shall have music wherever she goes.

DIDDLE, DIDDLE, DUMPLING

Diddle, diddle, dumpling, my son John,
Went to bed with his trousers on;
One shoe off and one shoe on,
Diddle, diddle, dumpling, my son John.

TO BED, TO BED

"To bed, to bed!" said Sleepy Head.
"Tarry a while," said Slow.
"Put on the pan," said Greedy Ann.
"We'll sup before we go."

THERE WAS A LITTLE GIRL

There was a little girl
And she had a little curl,
Right in the middle of her forehead;

When she was good,
She was very, very good,
But when she was bad,
She was horrid!

LADYBIRD, LADYBIRD

Ladybird, ladybird,
Fly away home.
Your house is on fire,
Your children are gone;

All except one,
And that's little Ann,
And she crept under
The warming pan.

THE LION AND THE UNICORN

The lion and the unicorn
Were fighting for the crown;
The lion beat the unicorn
All around the town.

Some gave them white bread,
And some gave them brown;
Some gave them plum cake,
And drummed them out of town.

WHAT ARE LITTLE GIRLS MADE OF?

What are little girls made of?
What are little girls made of?
Sugar and spice and all things nice,
That's what little girls are made of.

What are little boys made of?
What are little boys made of?
Snips and snails and puppy dogs' tails,
That's what little boys are made of.

HALF A POUND OF TUPPENNY RICE

Half a pound of tuppenny rice,
Half a pound of treacle,
That's the way the money goes,
Pop goes the weasel!

Up and down the city road,
In and out the Eagle,
That's the way the money goes,
Pop goes the weasel!

DING, DONG, BELL

Ding, dong, bell,
Pussy's in the well.
Who put her in?
Little Johnny Thin.

Who pulled her out?
Little Tommy Stout.
What a naughty boy was that
To try to drown poor pussycat,
Who never did him any harm,
But killed all the mice
In his father's barn.

ORANGES AND LEMONS

Oranges and lemons,
Say the bells of St. Clement's.
You owe me five farthings,
Say the bells of St Martin's.

When will you pay me?
Say the bells of Old Bailey.
When I grow rich,
Say the bells of Shoreditch.

When will that be?
Say the bells of Stepney.
I'm sure I don't know,
Says the great bell of Bow.

PEASE PUDDING

Pease pudding hot,
Pease pudding cold,
Pease pudding in the pot,
Nine days old.

YANKEE DOODLE

Yankee Doodle came to town,
Riding on a pony,
He stuck a feather in his cap,
And called it macaroni.